Be Caref

Written by Sally Murphy

Illustrated by Chantal Stewart

A mouse ran
down the path.
He was going
to the barn.

On his way,

he saw a dog.

"You are big,"

said the mouse.

"Be careful not

to step on me."

He saw a woolly sheep.

"You are big,"
said the mouse.

"Be careful not

to step on me."

7

He saw a goat
with long horns.
"You are big,"
said the mouse.
"Be careful not
to step on me."

9

He saw a brown cow.

"You are big,"

said the mouse.

"Be careful not

to step on me."

He saw a horse
with a white nose.
"You are *very* big,"
said the mouse.
"Be careful not
to step on me."

Then the mouse

saw an ant.

"You are very *little*,"

said the mouse.

"Be careful not
to step on me!"
said the ant.